BOOK • VIDEO

HOT LICKS

BUDDY GUY TEACHIN' THE BLUES

T0070808

To access video visit:
www.halleonard.com/mylibrary

Enter Code
1967-7121-8039-2582

ISBN: 978-1-5400-1376-7

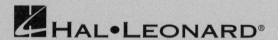

Visit Hal Leonard Online at
www.halleonard.com

Contact us:
Hal Leonard
7777 West Bluemound Road
Milwaukee, WI 53213
Email: info@halleonard.com

In Europe, contact:
Hal Leonard Europe Limited
42 Wigmore Street
Marylebone, London, W1U 2RN
Email: info@halleonardeurope.com

In Australia, contact:
Hal Leonard Australia Pty. Ltd.
4 Lentara Court
Cheltenham, Victoria, 3192 Australia
Email: info@halleonard.com.au

CONTENTS

Outro and Credits

BIOGRAPHY

With his inventive and signature electric guitar style, George "Buddy" Guy has come to symbolize traditional Chicago blues.

Guy was born on July 30, 1936, into a sharecropping family in Lettsworth, Louisiana, where he picked cotton until blues songs on the radio inspired him to take up guitar. He started out in the early 1950s playing local roadhouses in Baton Rouge, and in 1957 moved to Chicago's thriving south side.

Guy immersed himself in the Windy City's blues scene, quickly gaining renown in "head-cutting" competitions against Otis Rush and Magic Sam—who introduced Guy to Cobra Records' Eli Toscano. Guy recorded two singles for Cobra in 1958.

Guy soon moved to Chess Records (the famed label which had already recorded with Howlin' Wolf and Muddy Waters), where he recorded some of his trademark songs, including "First Time I Met the Blues" and Willie Dixon's "Let Me Love You Baby."

Nearly a decade later, Guy moved to Vanguard and formed a partnership with harpist Junior Wells. The pair recorded *Buddy Guy and Junior Wells Play the Blues*, in 1972, as well as a live recording from the Montreux Jazz Festival, titled *Drinkin' TNT 'n' Smokin' Dynamite*.

Guy continued to live in Chicago, making his living as the owner of the Checkerboard Lounge before opening his now-famous Buddy Guy's Legends blues club in 1989. His first three albums for Silvertone in the 1990s all earned Grammy awards, and his fame spread far beyond the Chicago blues scene.

In 2005, Guy was inducted into the Rock and Roll Hall of Fame, and today is held in the same esteem as blues guitar legends B.B. King, Eric Clapton, Jimi Hendrix, and his old friend Stevie Ray Vaughan. Guy continues to tour and perform on a regular basis. To learn more, visit *BuddyGuy.net*.

SELECTED DISCOGRAPHY

I Left My Blues in San Francisco (Chess, 1967)

A Man and the Blues (Vanguard, 1968)

Blues Today (Vanguard, 1968)

This Is Buddy Guy (Vanguard, 1968)

Buddy and the Juniors (MCA, 1970)

Buddy & Junior Mance & Junior Wells (Harvest, 1971)

In the Beginning (1958/1961) (Drive, 1971)

Buddy Guy and Junior Wells Play the Blues (Rhino, 1972)

Hold That Plane (Vanguard, 1972)

Live in Montreux (Evidence, 1977)

Pleading the Blues (Evidence, 1979)

Buddy Guy & Phil Guy (JSP, 1979)

Got to Use Your Head (Blues Ball, 1979)

The Dollar Done Fell (JSP, 1980)

Stone Crazy! (Alligator, 1981)

DJ Play My Blues (JSP, 1982)

Drinkin' TNT 'n' Smokin' Dynamite (Blind Pig, 1982)

Buddy Guy (Chess, 1983)

Damn Right I've Got the Blues (Silvertone, 1991)

Sweet Tea (Silvertone/Jive, 2001)

Chapter 1: John Lee Hooker and Blues in E

Example 1

(4:29)

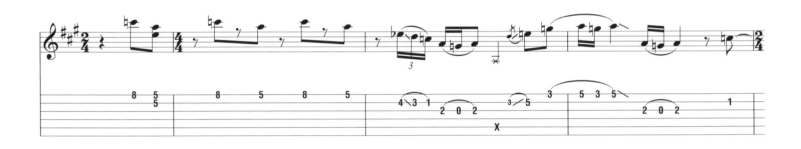

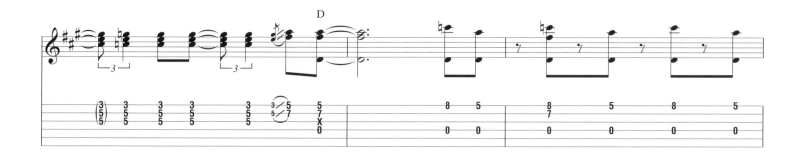

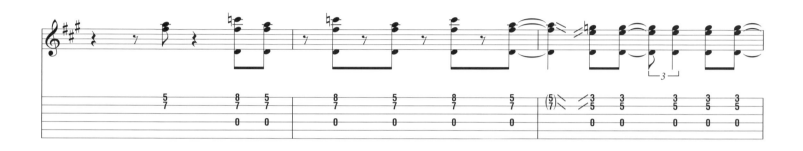

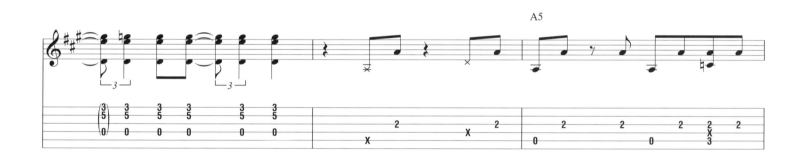

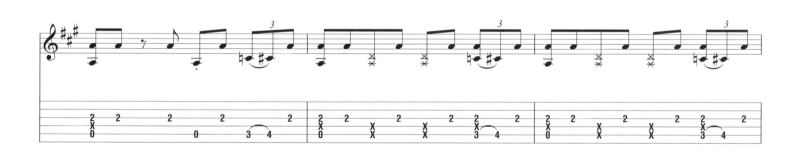

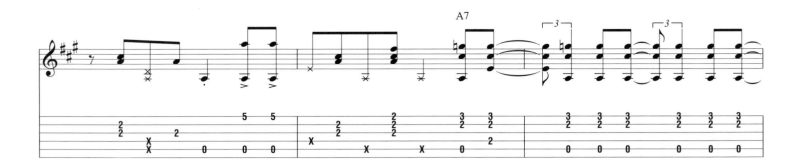

A7

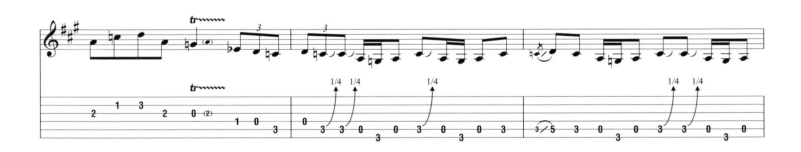

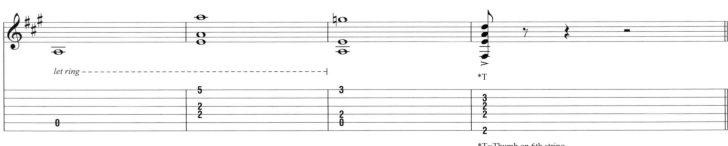

*T=Thumb on 6th string

Example 2

(6:50)

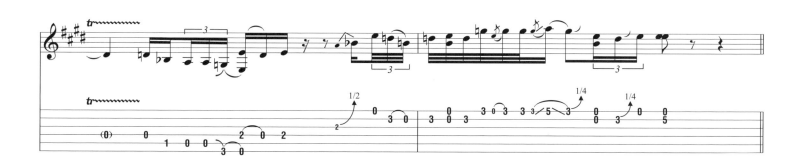

9

Example 3
(7:50)

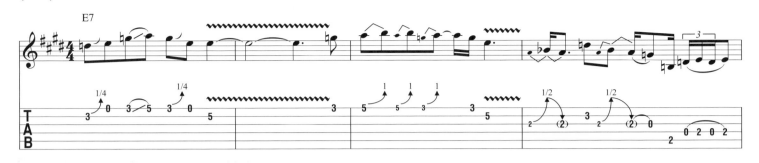

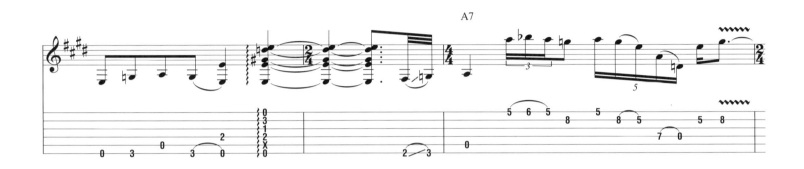

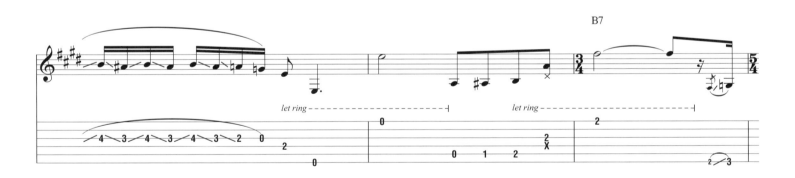

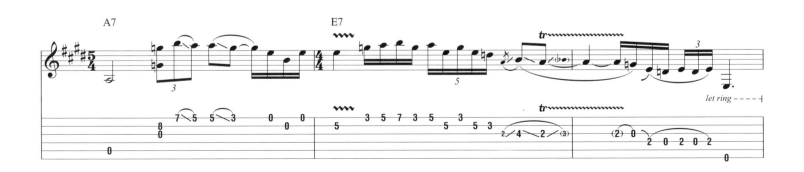

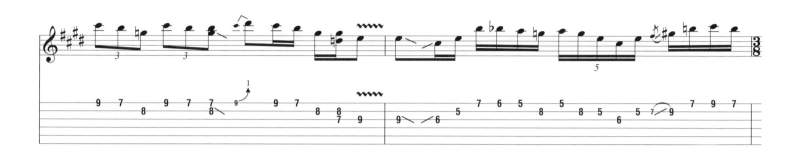

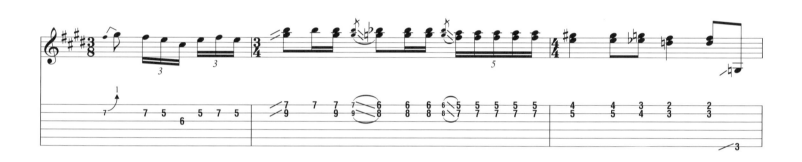

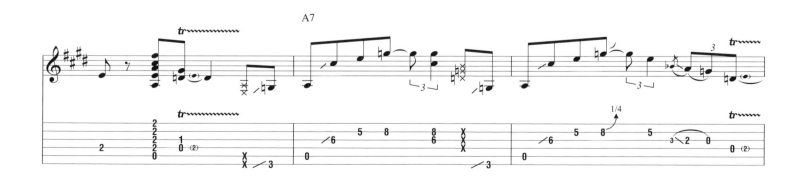

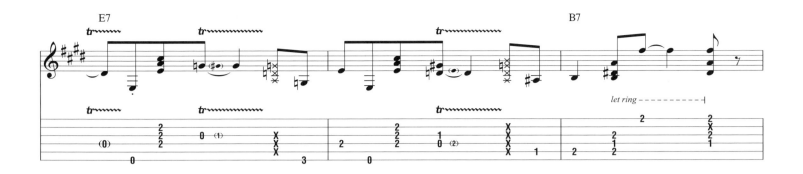

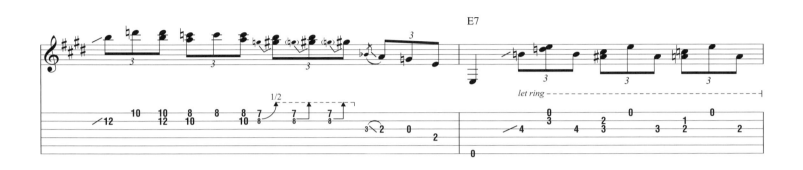

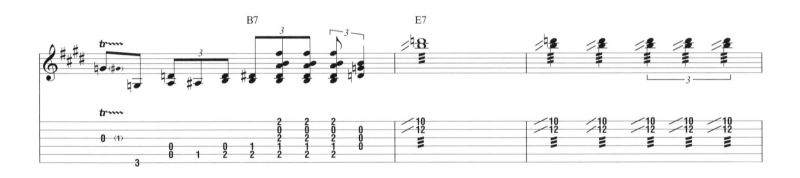

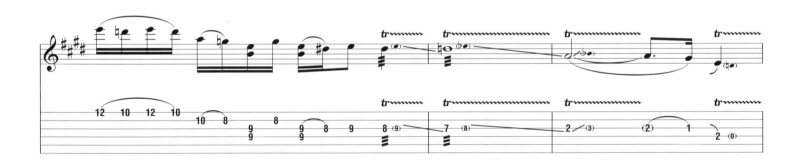

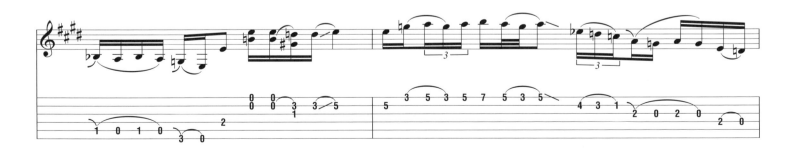

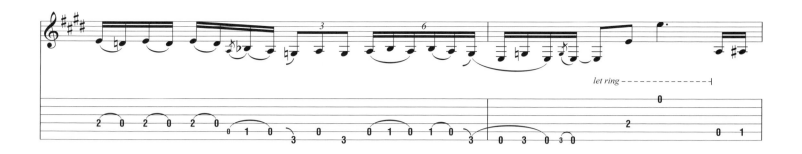

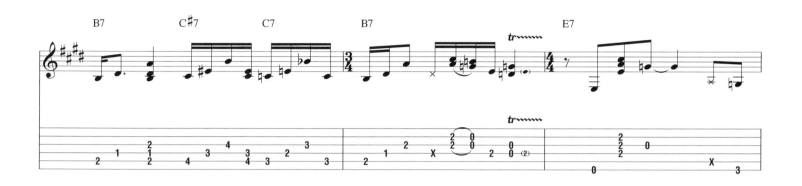

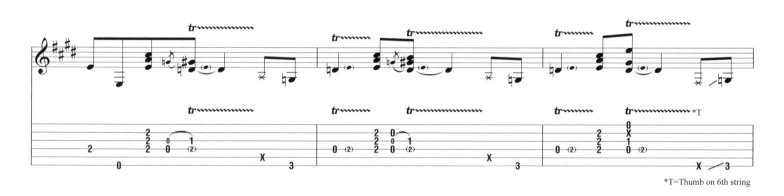

*T=Thumb on 6th string

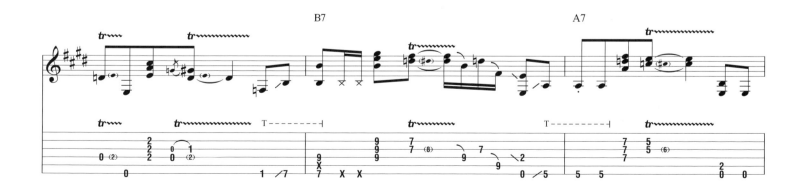

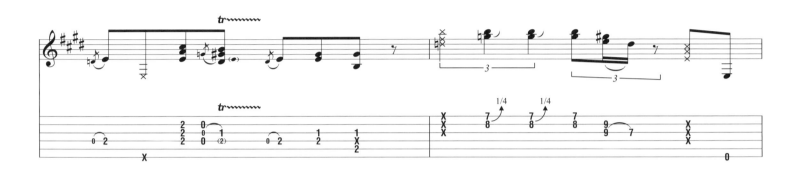

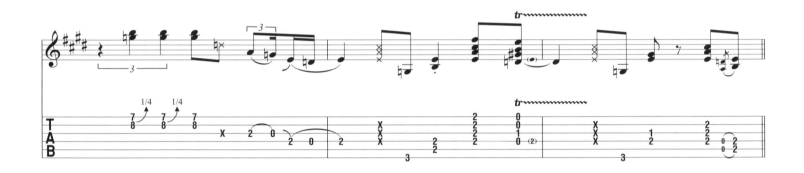

Example 4
(10:54)

*T=Thumb on 6th string

Chapter 2: Blues in A

Example 5

(:00)

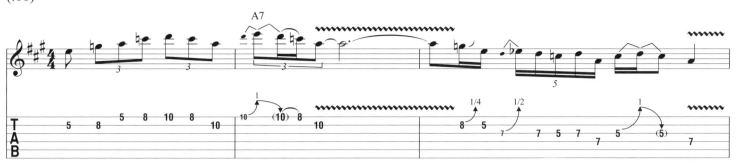

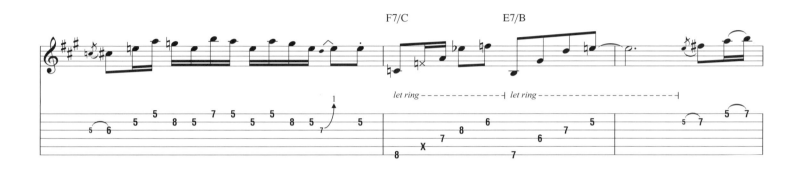

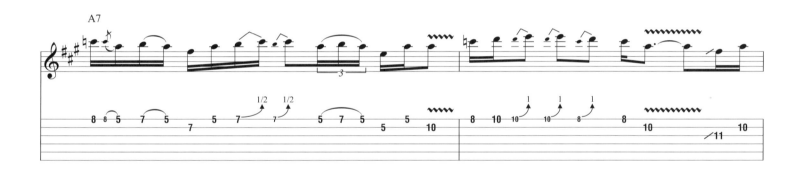

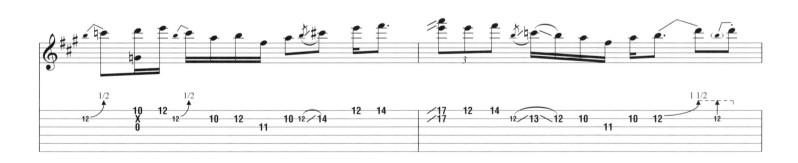

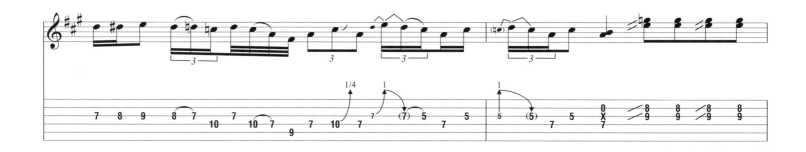

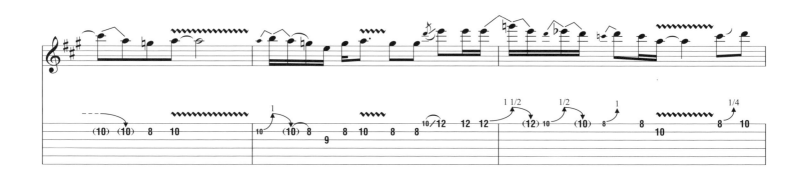

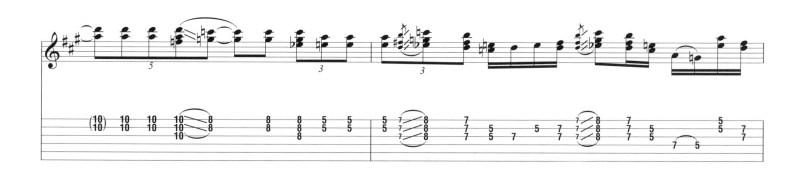

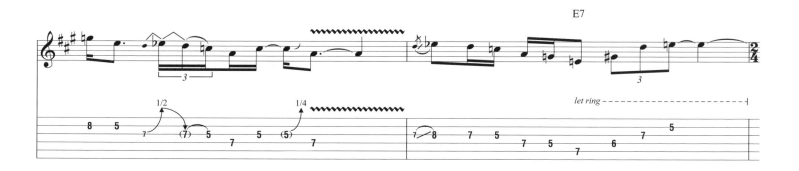

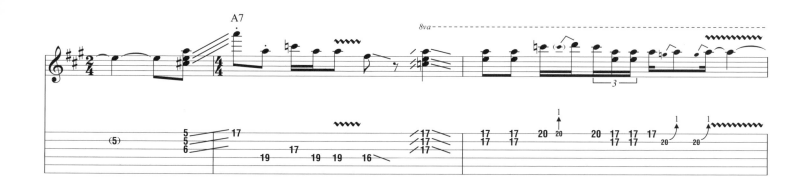

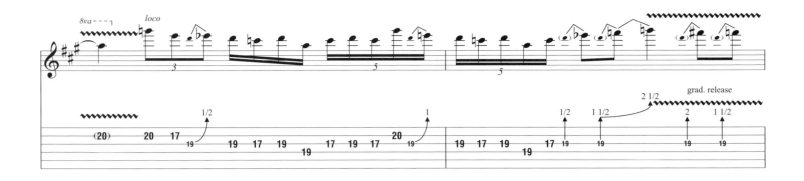

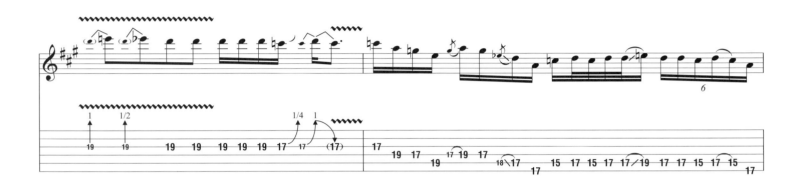

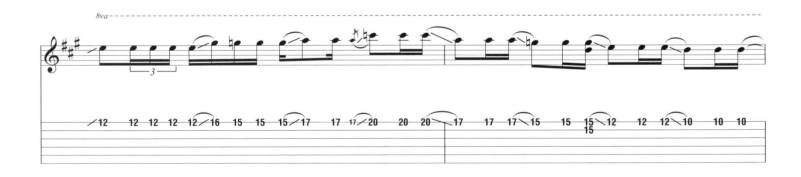

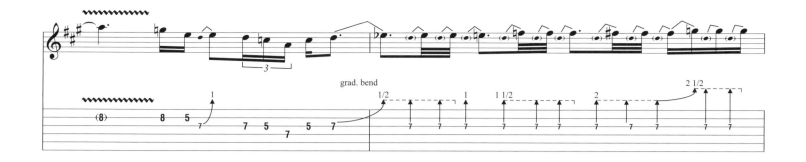

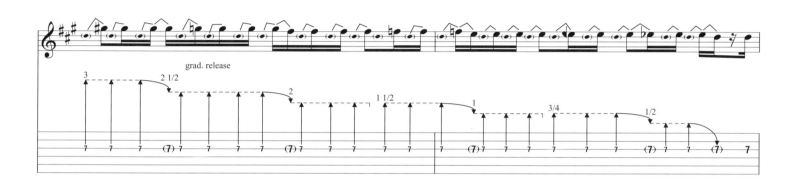

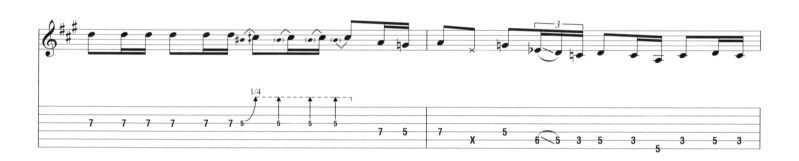

Example 6
(2:29)

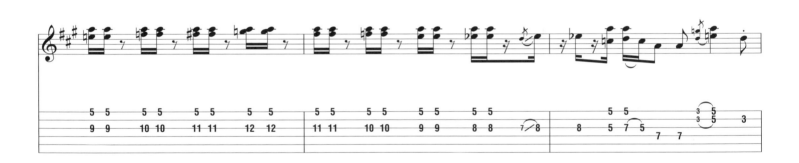

Example 7
(2:56)

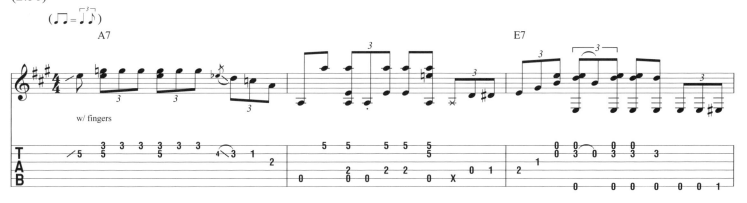

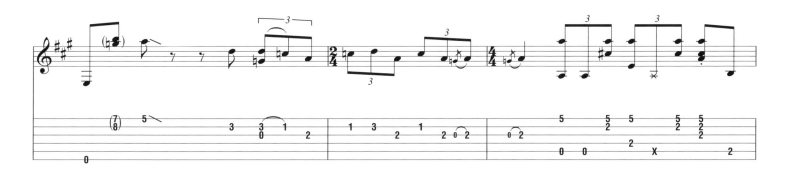

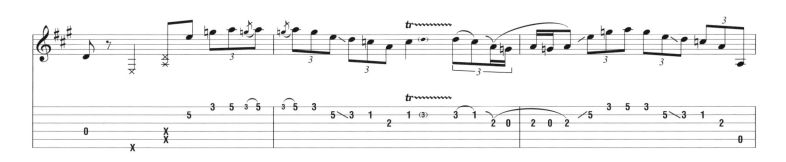

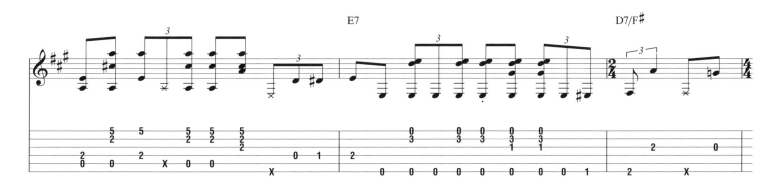

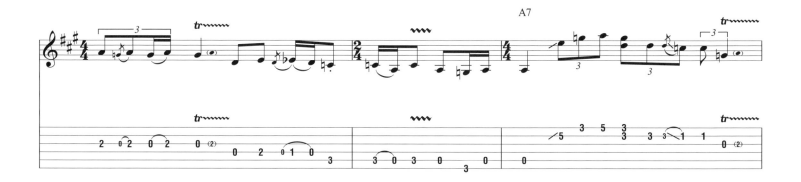

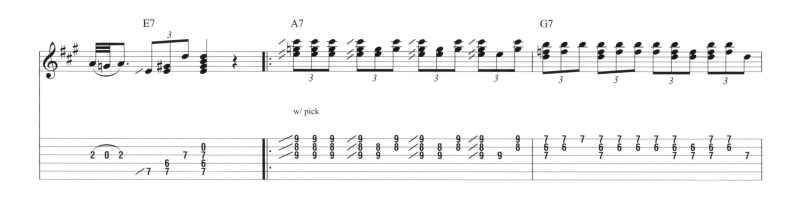

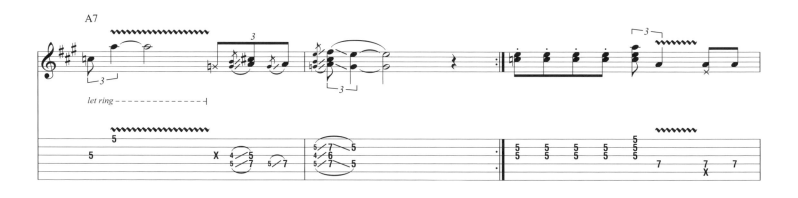

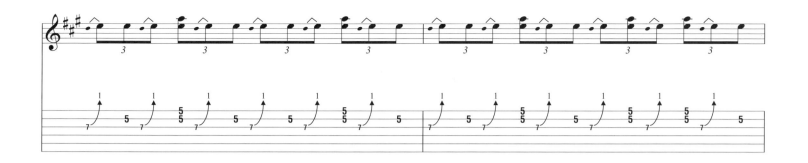

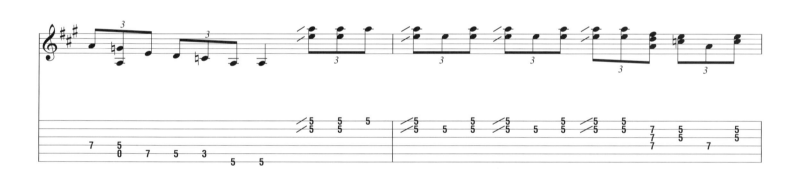

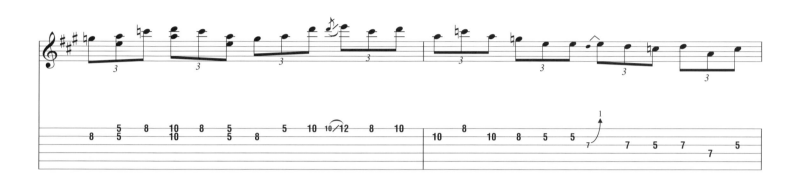

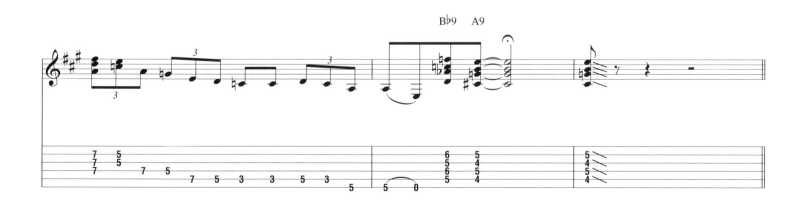

Chapter 3: Jimmy Reed Style

Example 8

(:30)

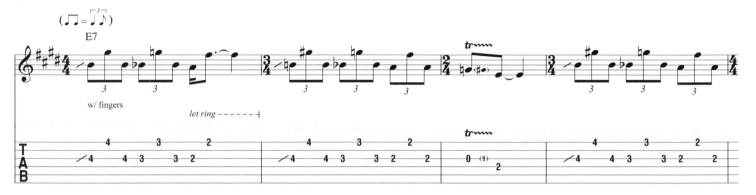

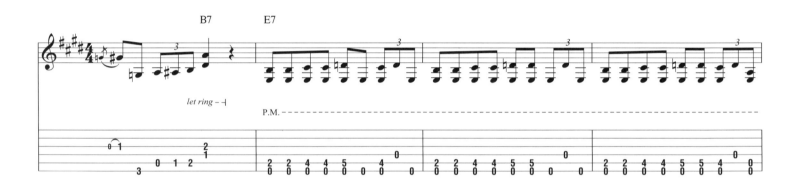

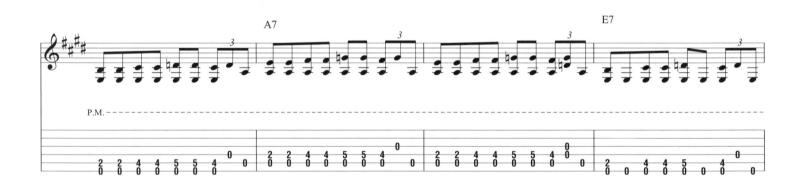

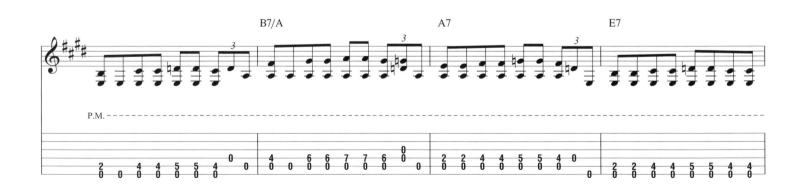

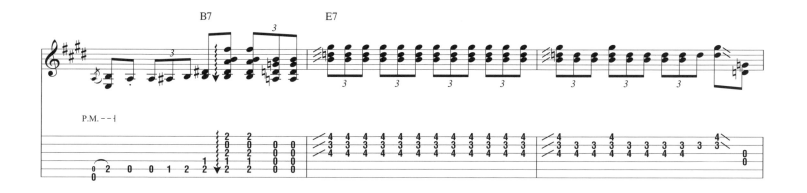

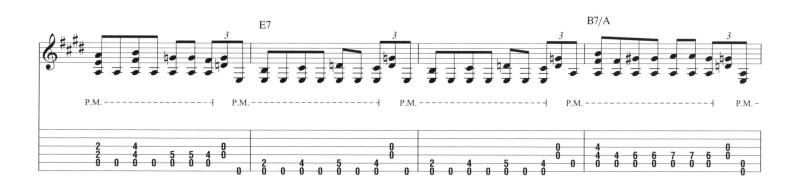

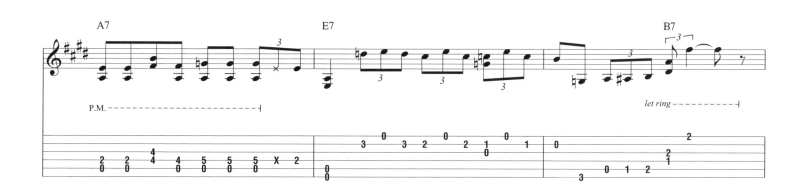

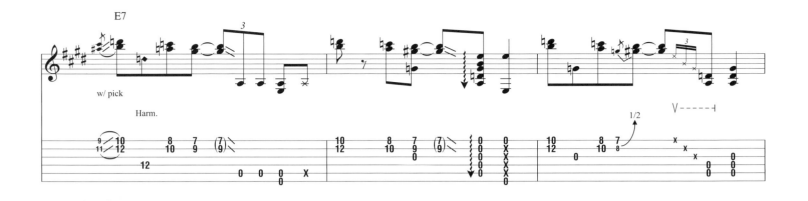

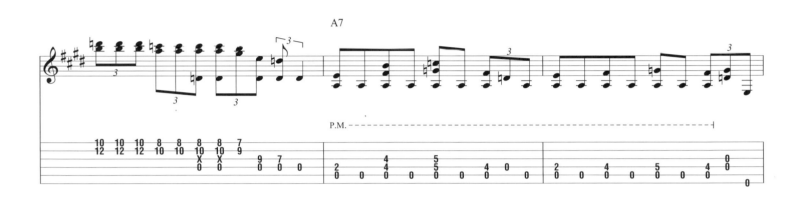

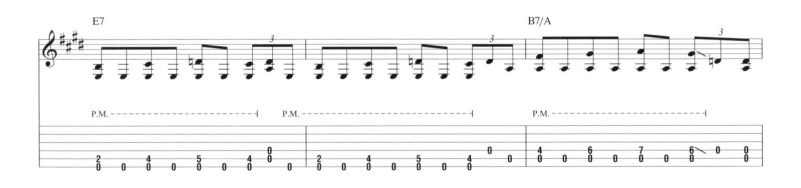

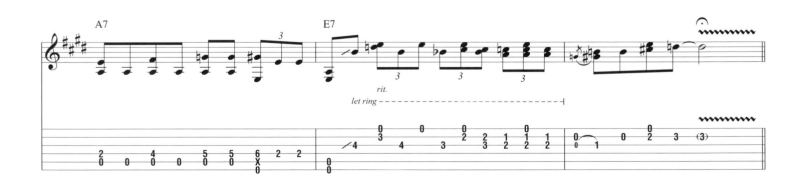

Chapter 4: T-Bone Walker Chords and Classic Riffs

Example 9
(:26)

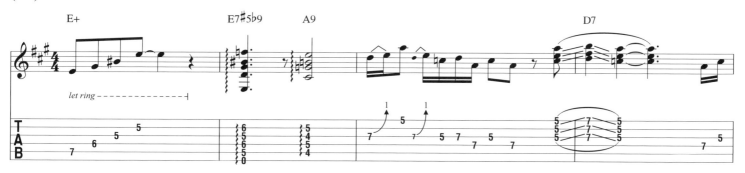

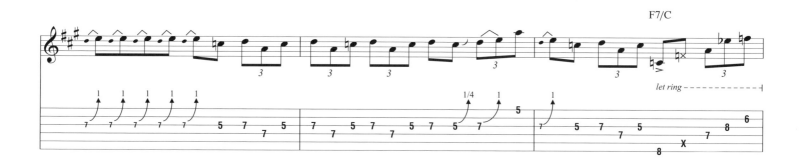

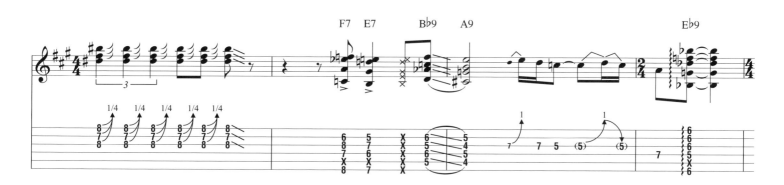

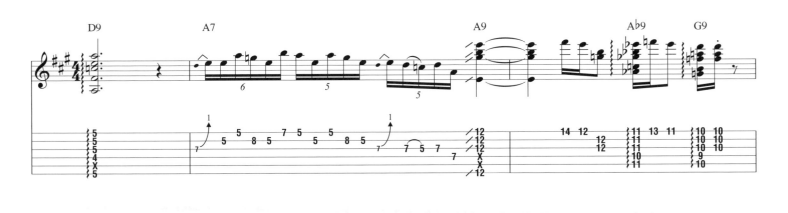

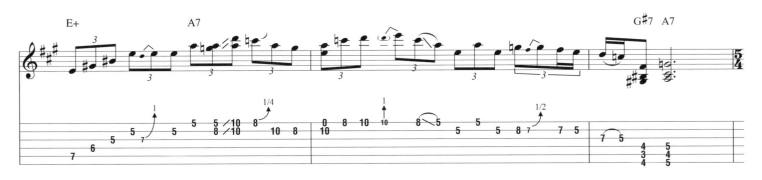

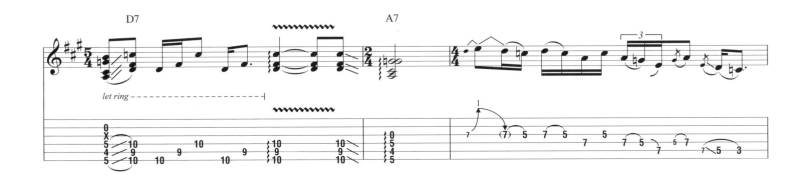

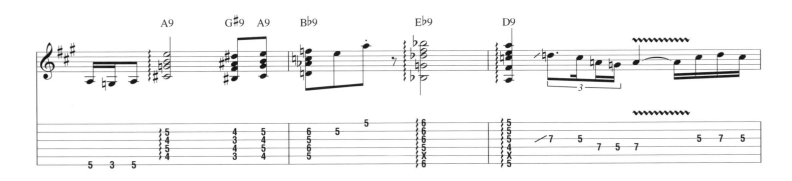

Example 10
(2:08)

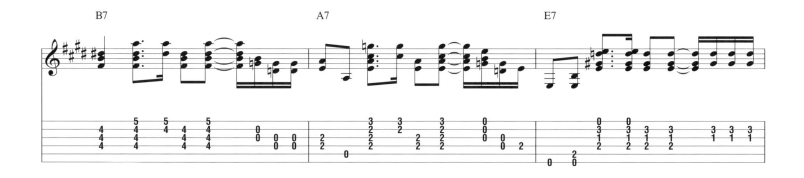

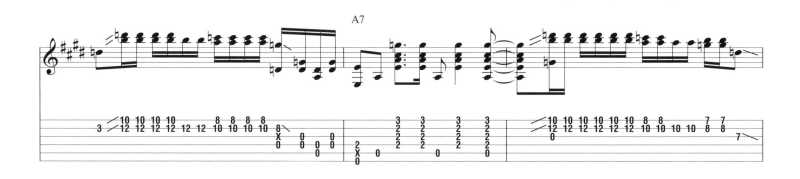

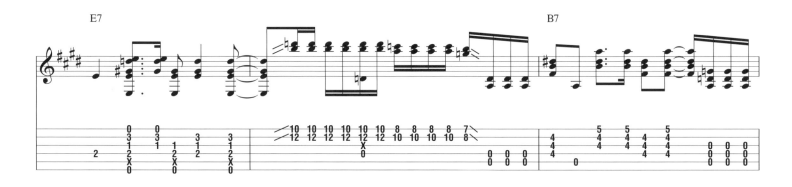

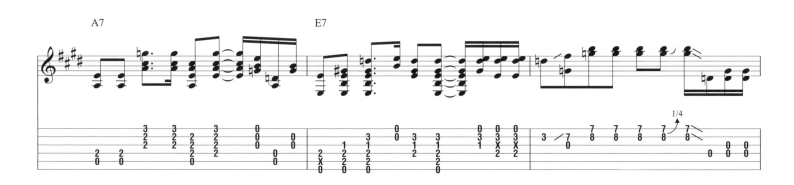

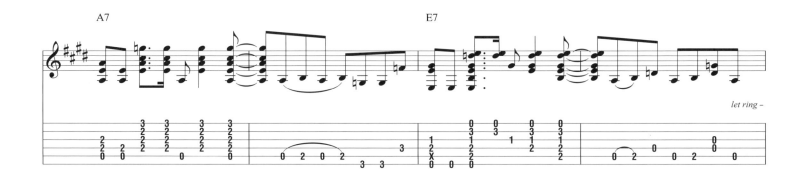

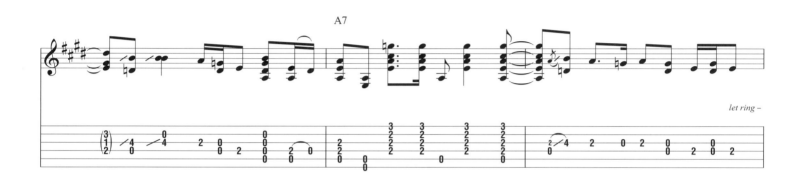

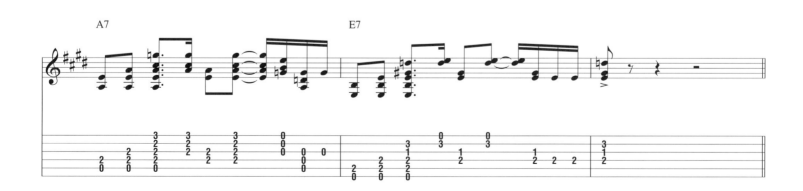

Example 11
(3:36)

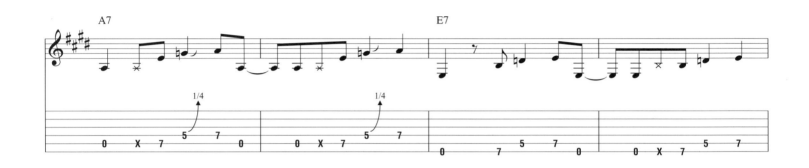

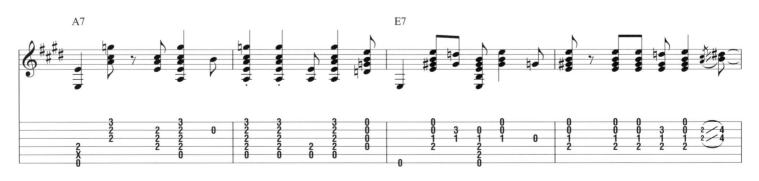

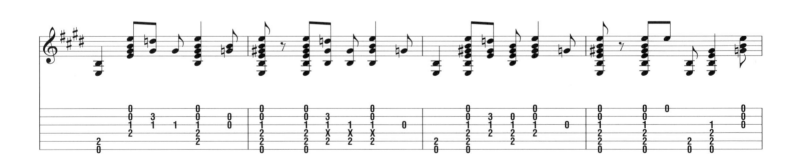

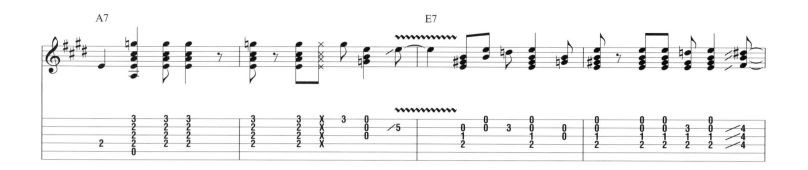

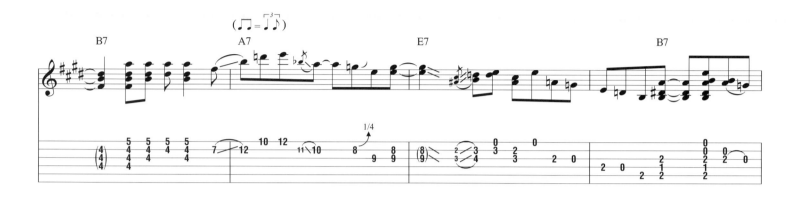

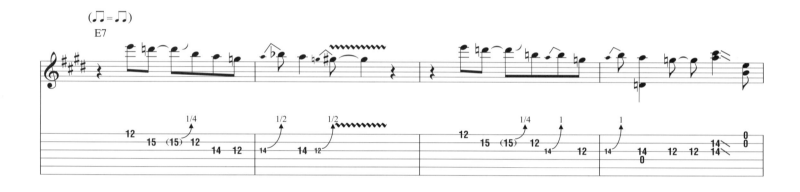

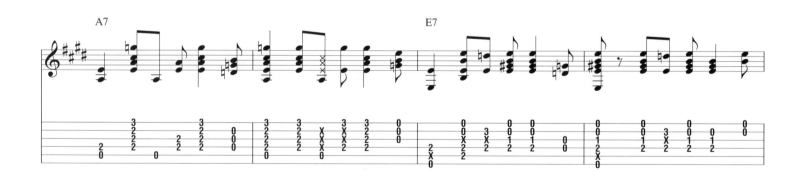

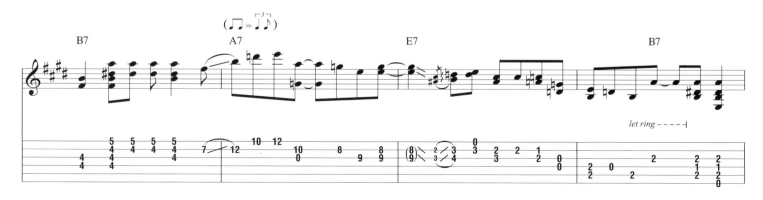

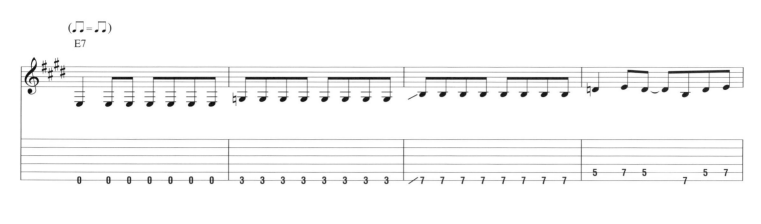

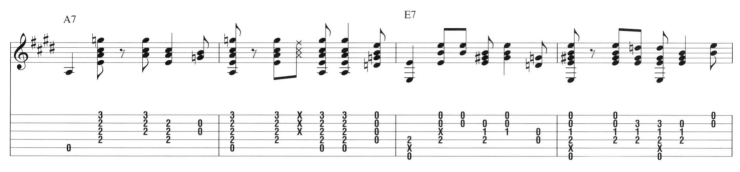

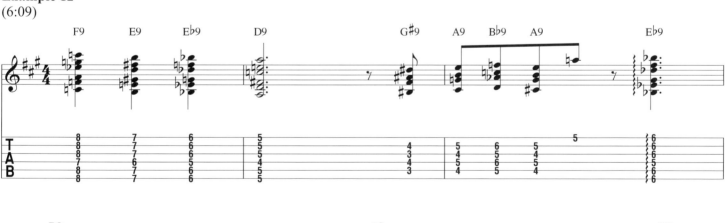

Example 12
(6:09)

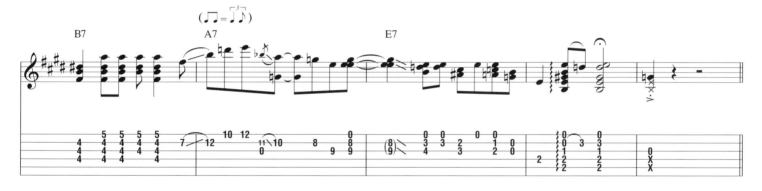

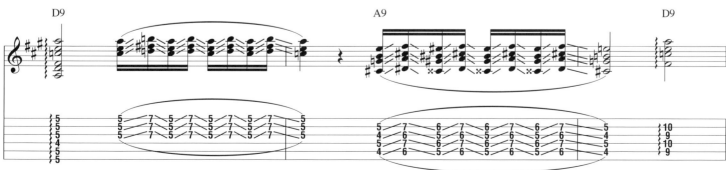

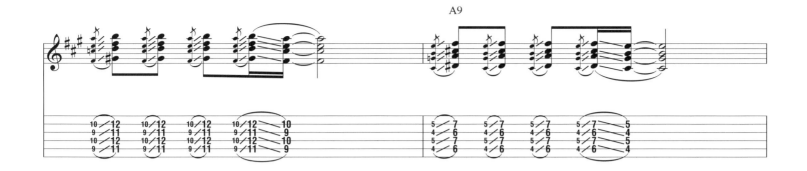

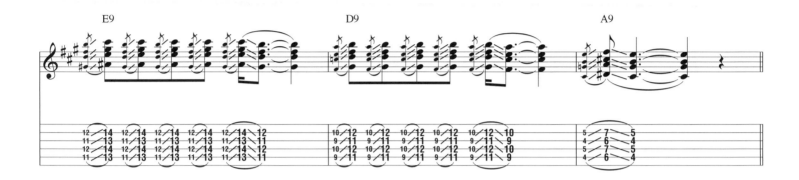

Example 13
(7:41)

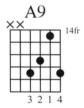 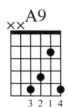

Example 14
(8:57)

Chapter 5: Little Walter and Jazz Piano Rhythms

Example 15

(:27)

Example 16
(1:11)

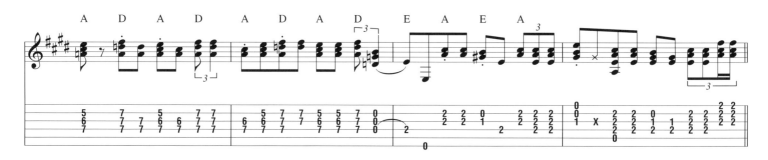

Example 17
(2:00)

Example 18
(2:34)

Example 19

(2:53)

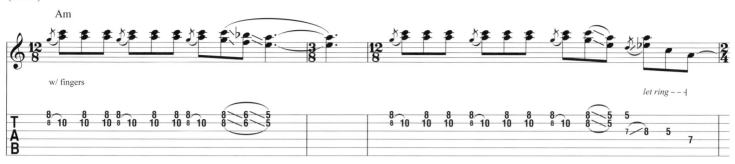

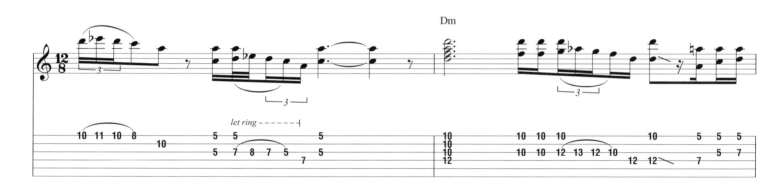

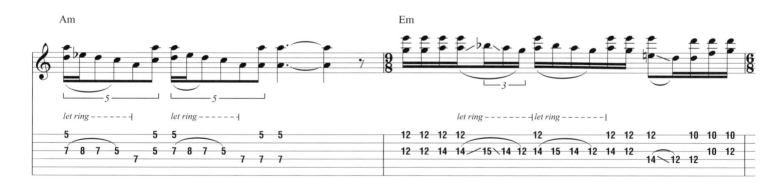

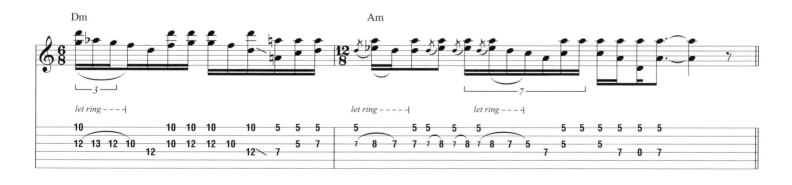

39

Chapter 6: Using a Pick or Fingers

Example 20
(:27)

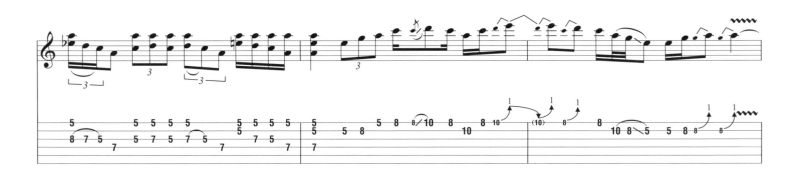

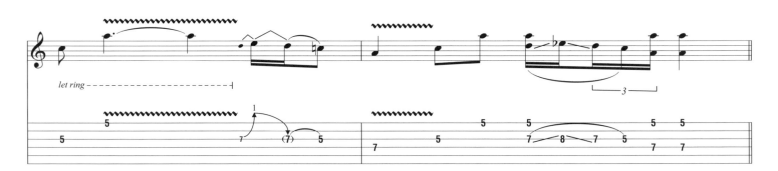

Example 21

(:55)

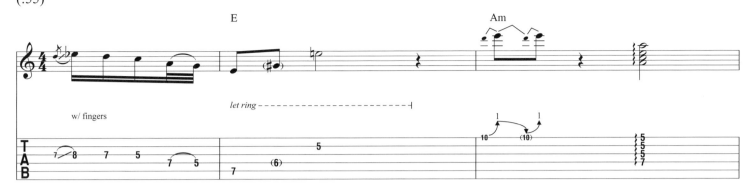

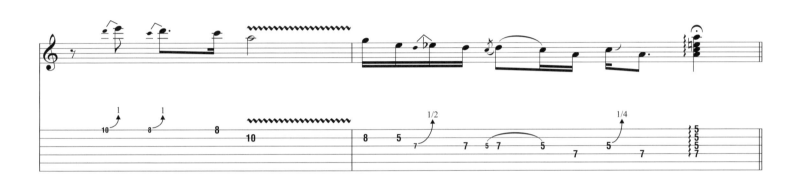

Chapter 7: Emulating Slide Guitar

Example 22

(:12)

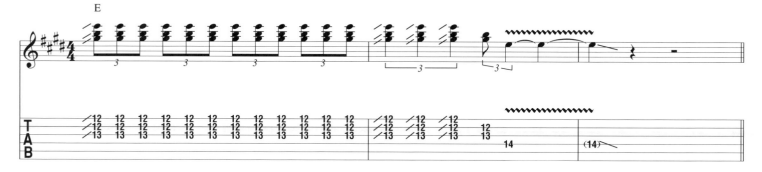

Example 23

(:26)

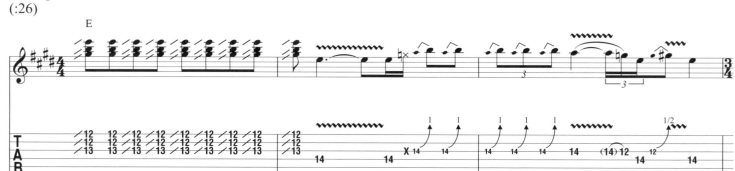

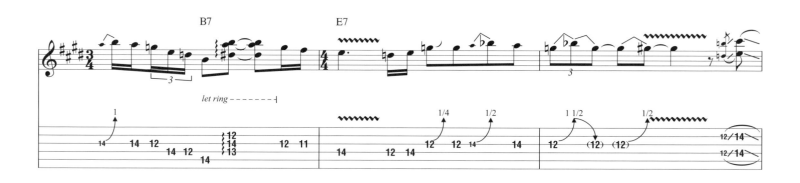

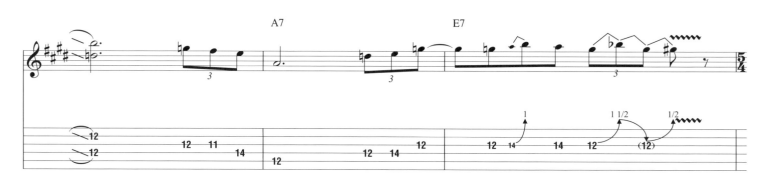

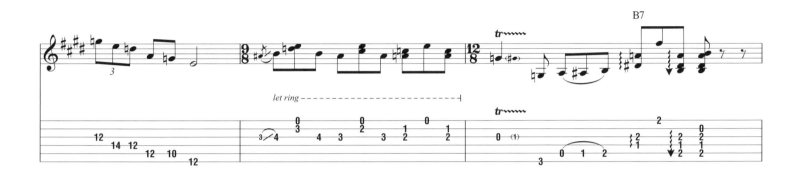

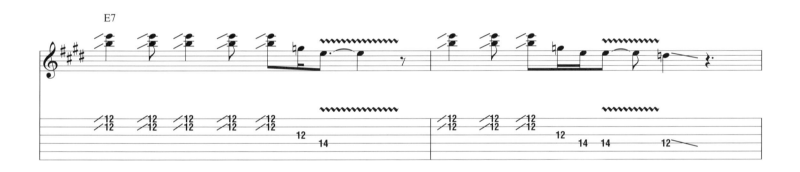

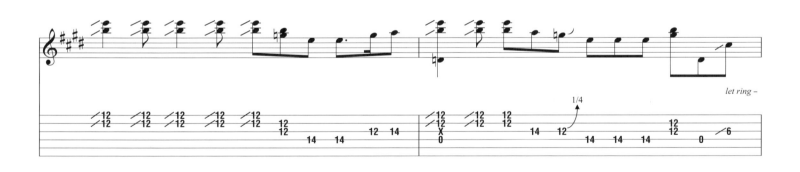

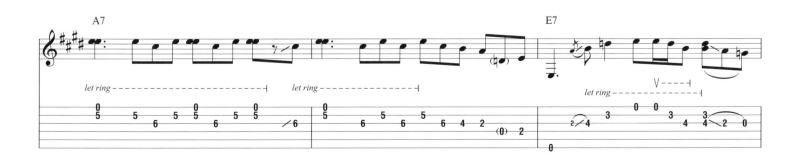

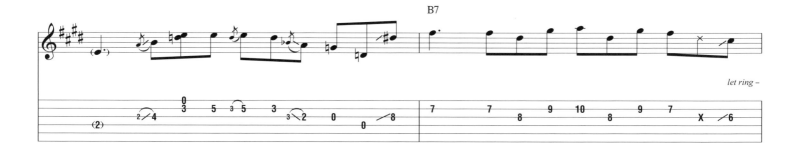

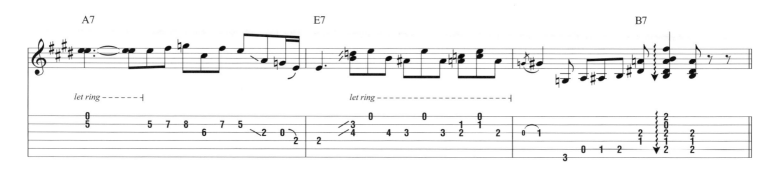

Example 24
(1:58)

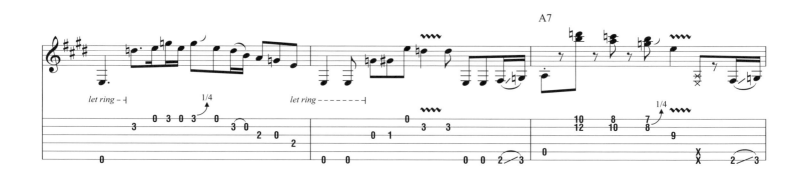

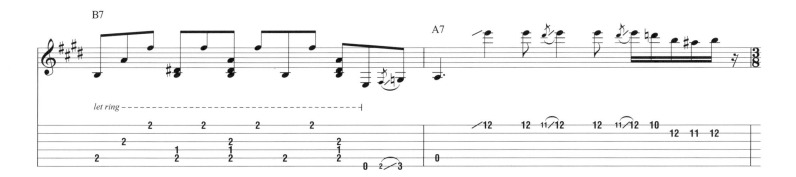

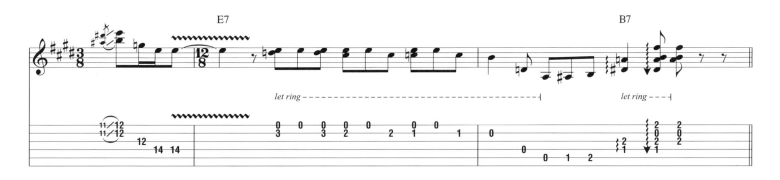

Example 25
(2:53)

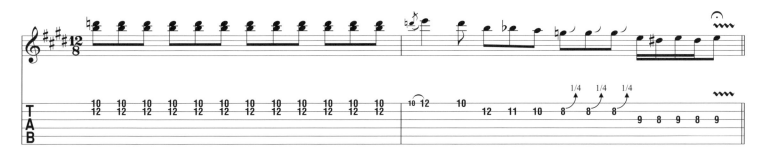

Example 26
(3:07)

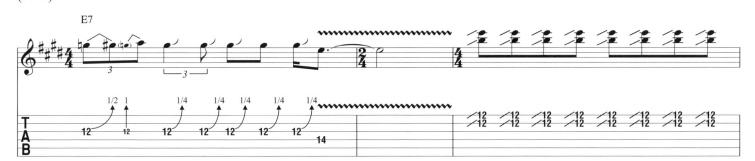

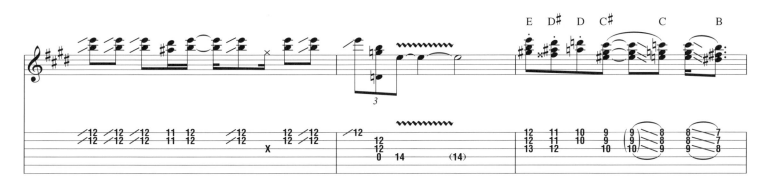

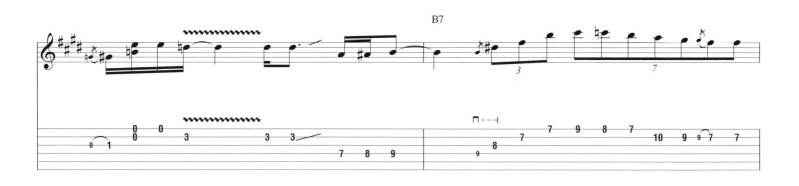

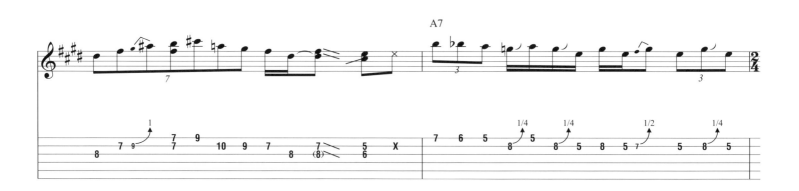

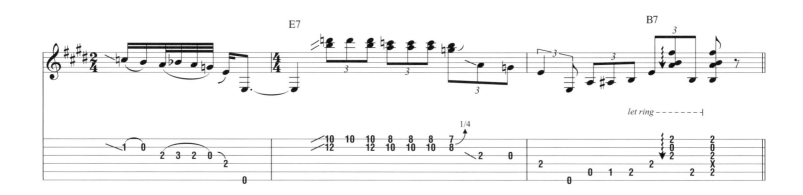

Chapter 8: Boogie Riffs and a Turnaround

Example 27
(:12)

Example 28

(:40)

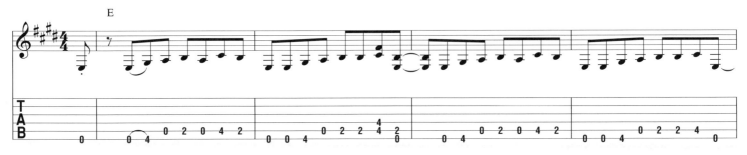

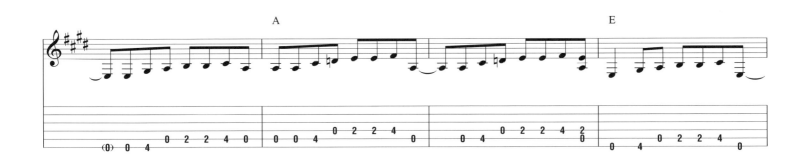

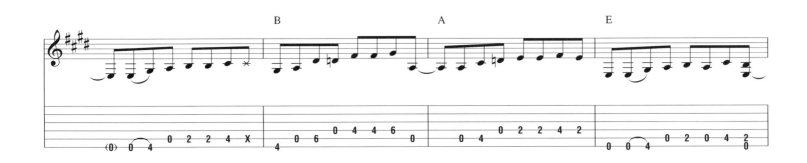

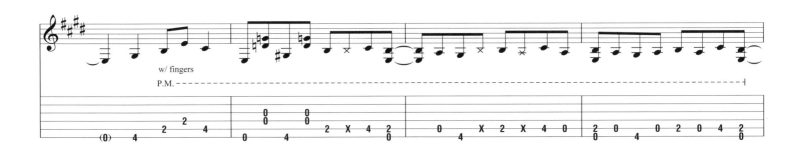

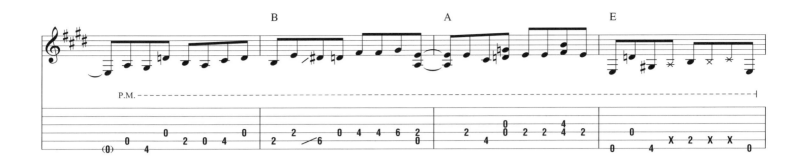

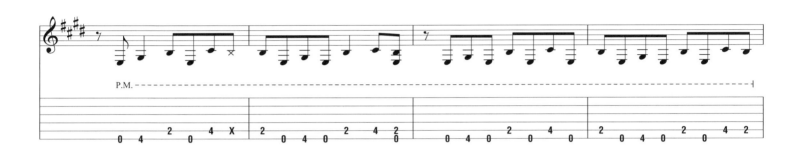

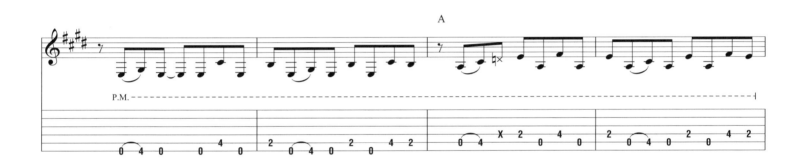

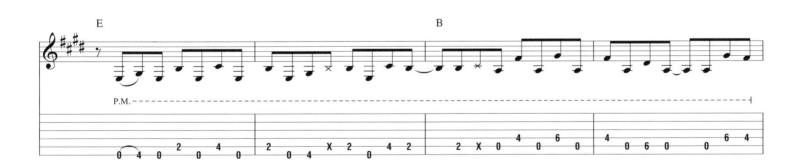

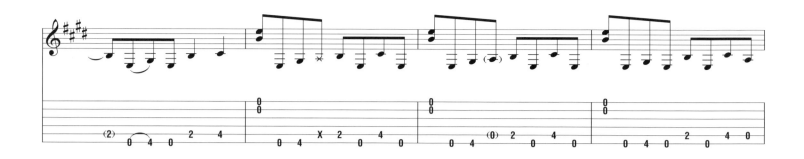

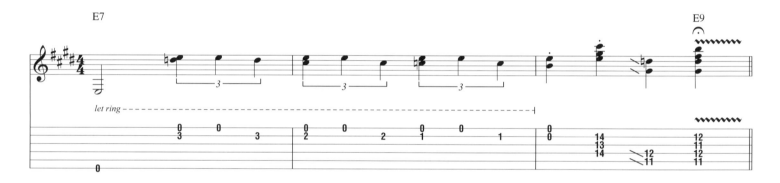

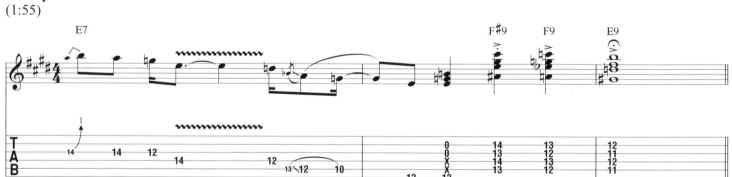

Example 29
(1:55)

Example 30
(3:19)

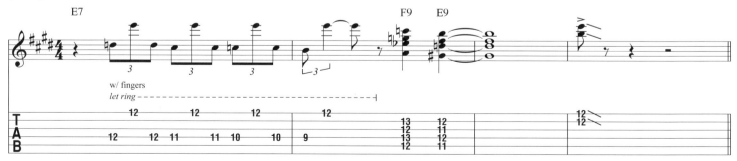

Chapter 9: Tone - String Gauge and Pick v. Fingers

*Tune down 1 step:
 (low to high) D-G-C-F-A-D

*Examples 31-34

Example 31

(3:46)

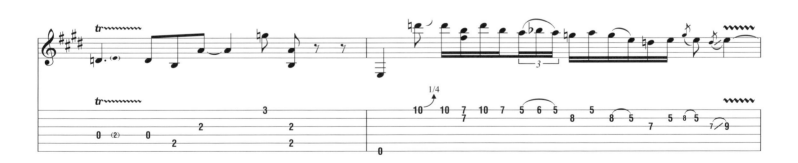

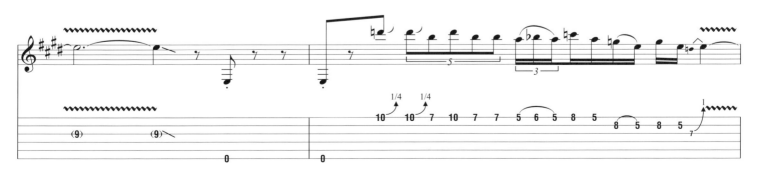

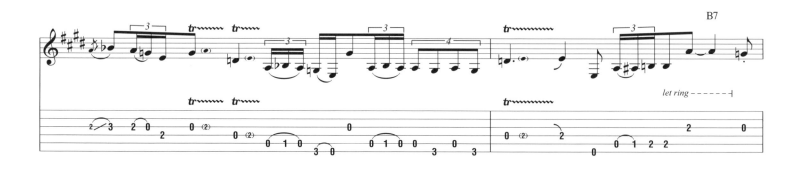

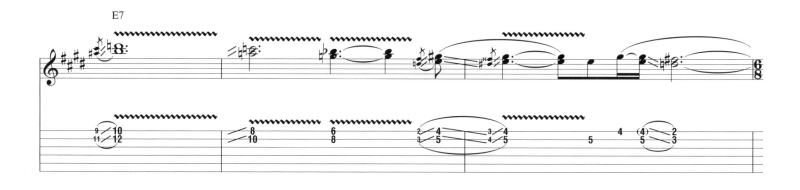

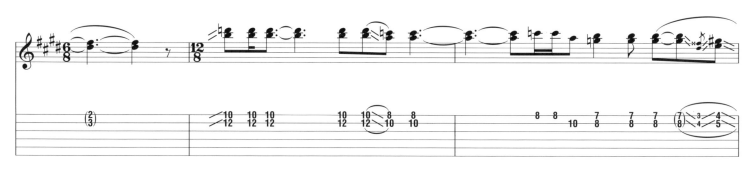

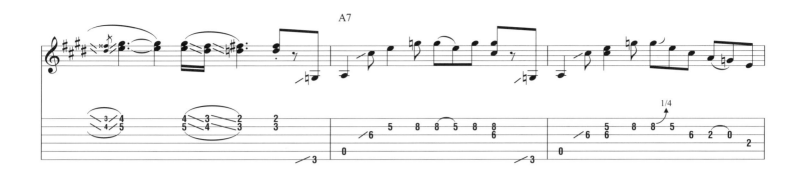

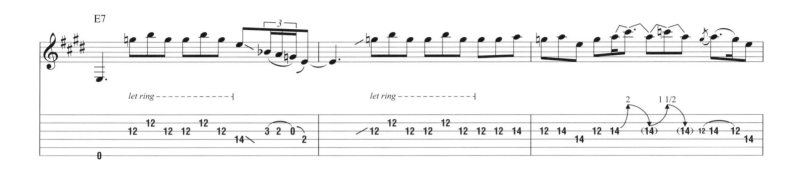

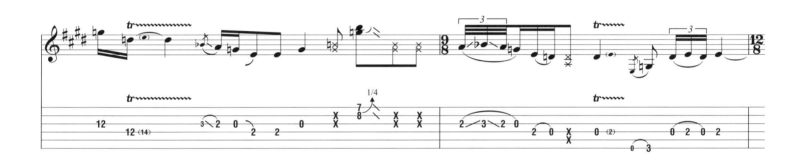

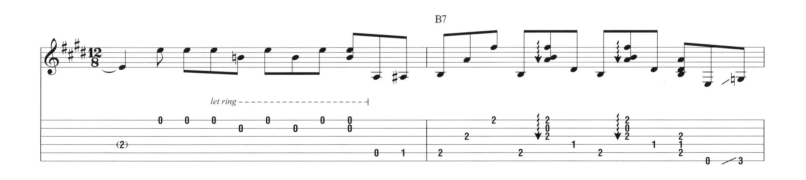

Example 32

(7:31)

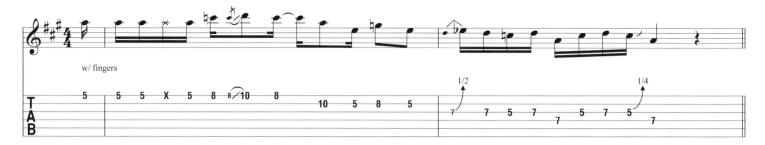

Example 33

(7:51)

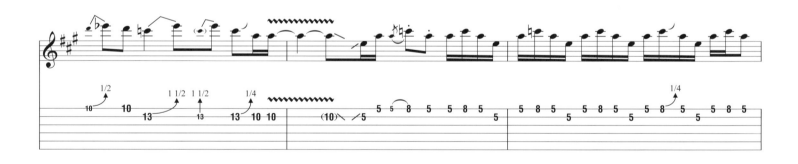

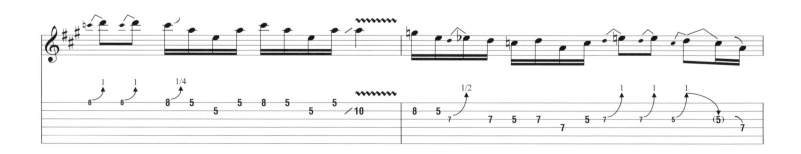

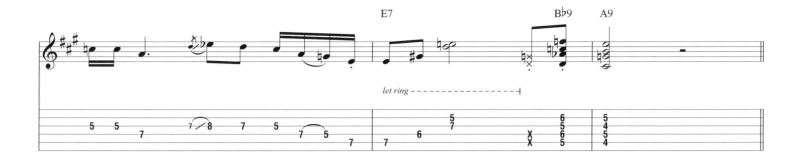

Example 34
(8:39)

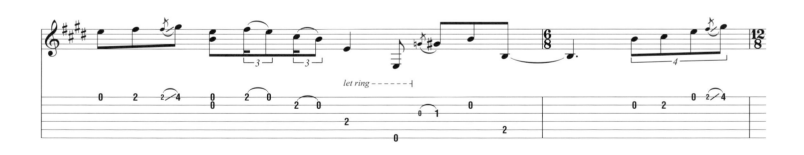

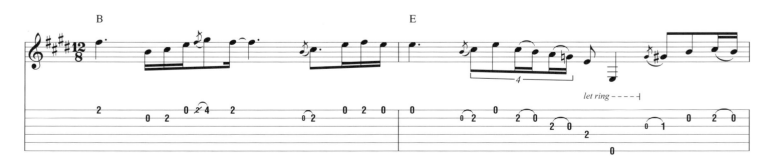

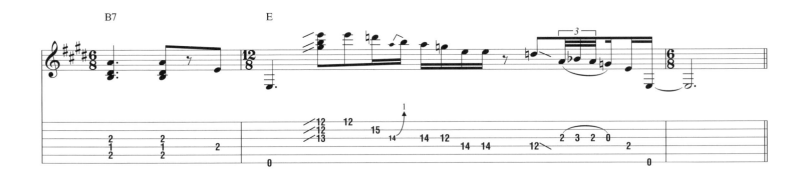

Chapter 10: Stealing Licks – The Buddy Guy Sound

*Tune down 1 step:
(low to high) D-G-C-F-A-D

*Examples 35 & 36

Example 35
(2:42)

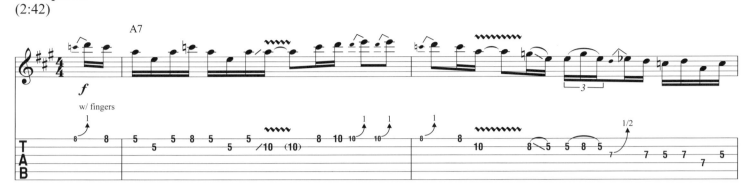

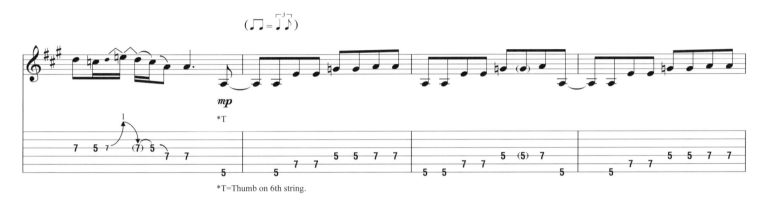

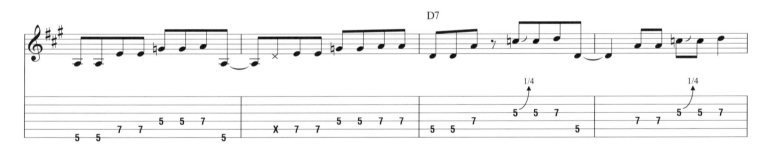

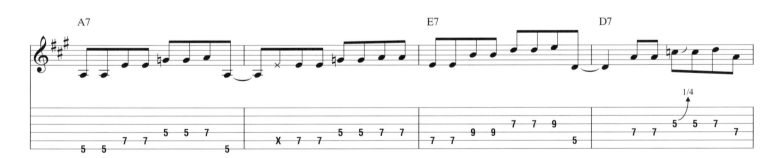

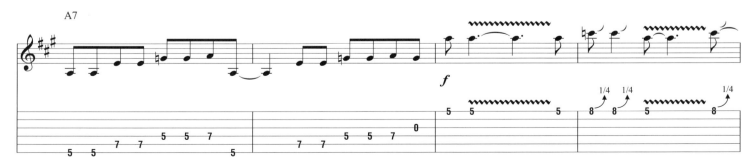

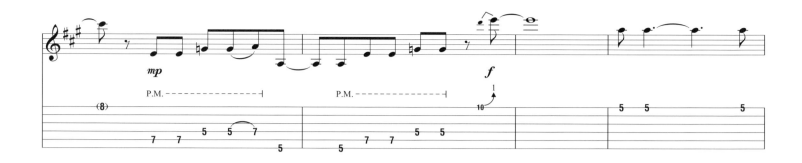

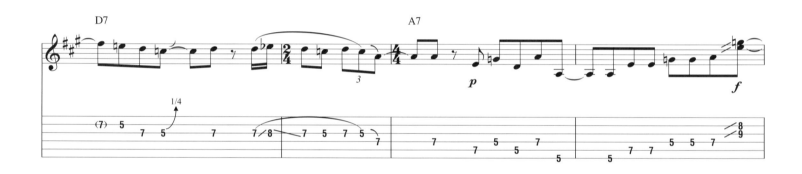

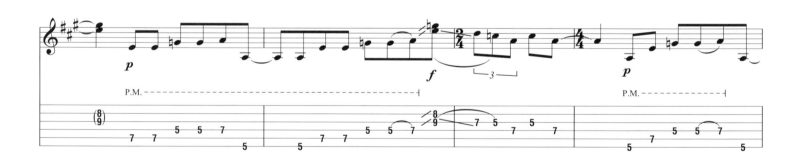

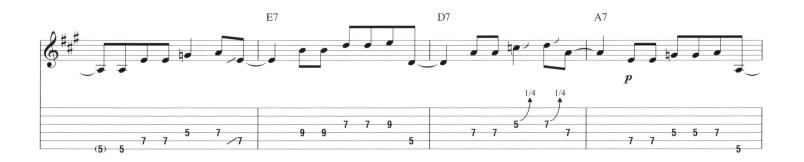

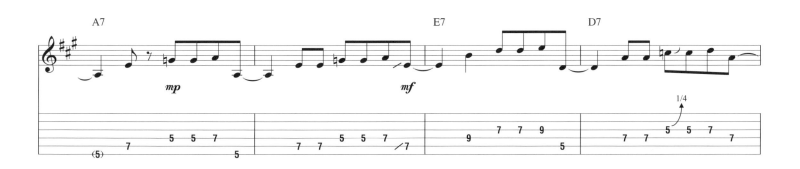

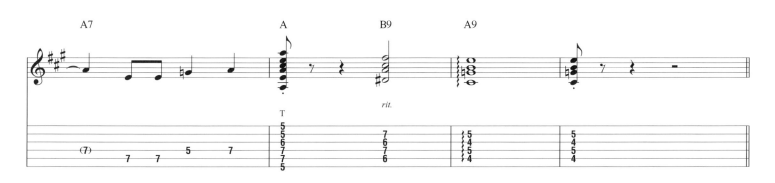

Example 36
(5:05)

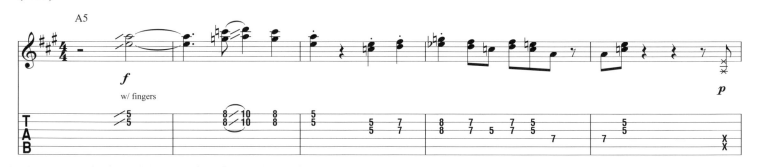

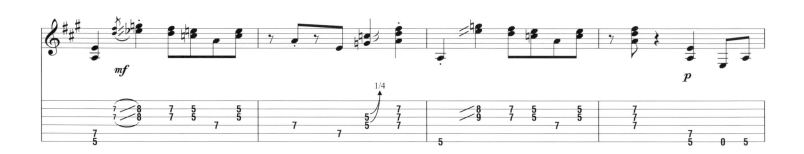

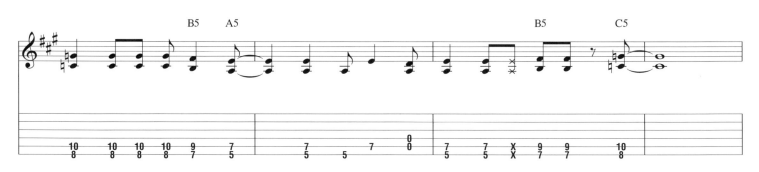

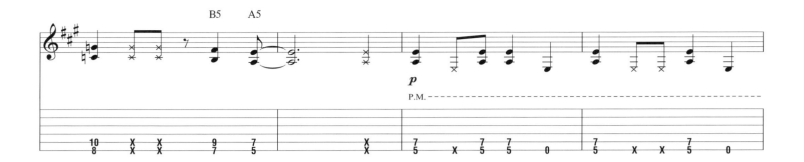

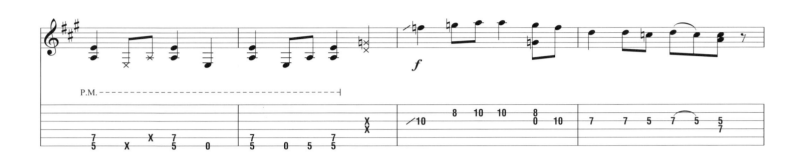

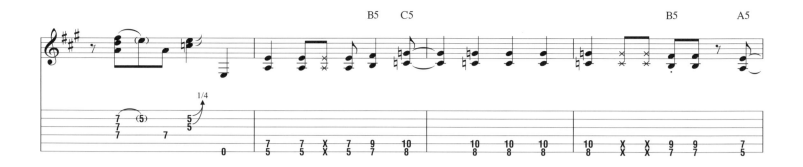

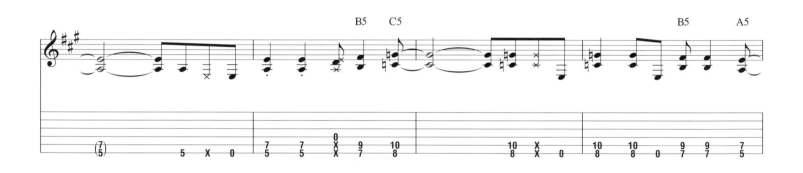

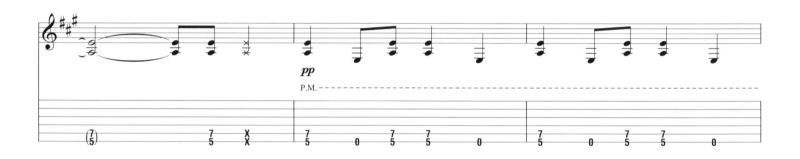

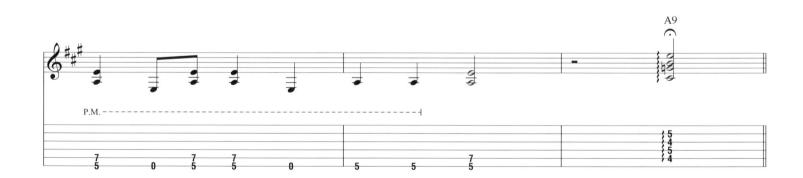

Chapter 11: Drop D Tuning

Example 37
(:26)

Drop D tuning, down 1 step:
(low to high) C-G-C-F-A-D

w/ fingers
let ring throughout

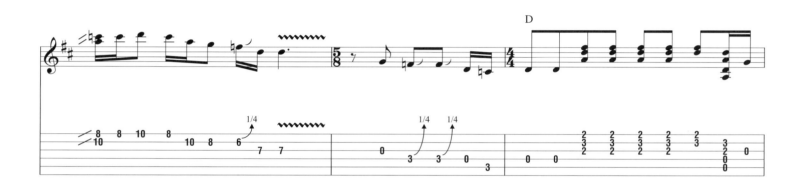

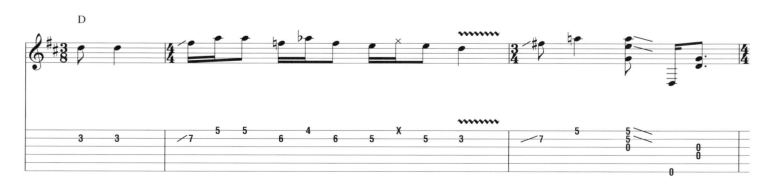

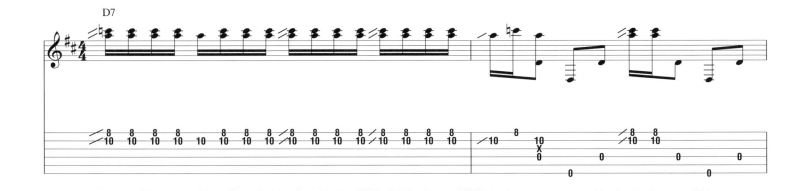

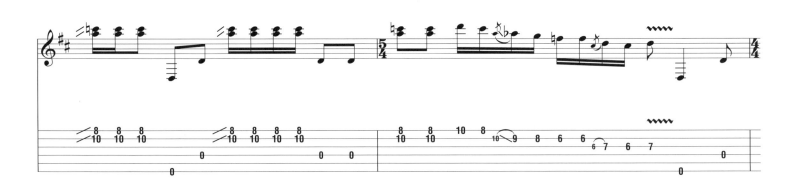

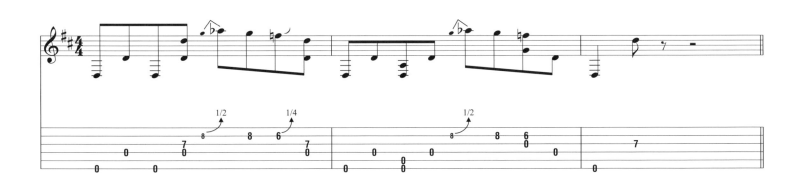

Chapter 12: Lightnin' Hopkins

*Tune down 1 step:
(low to high) D-G-C-F-A-D

*Examples 38 - 40

Example 38

(:13)

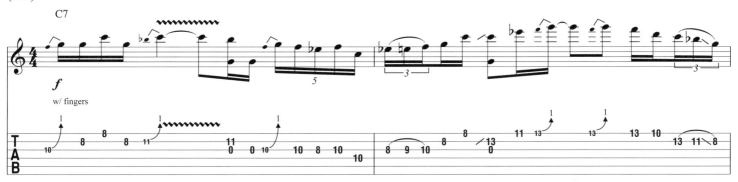

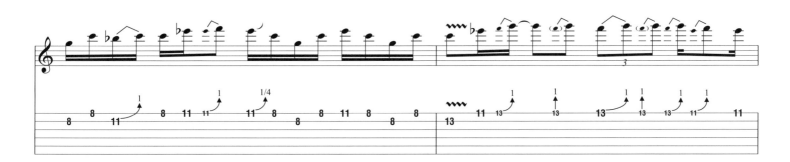

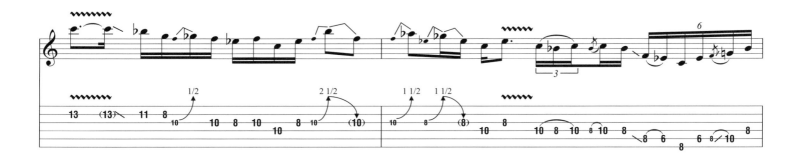

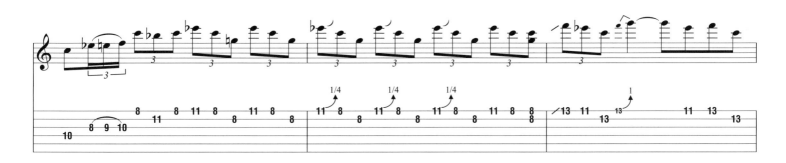

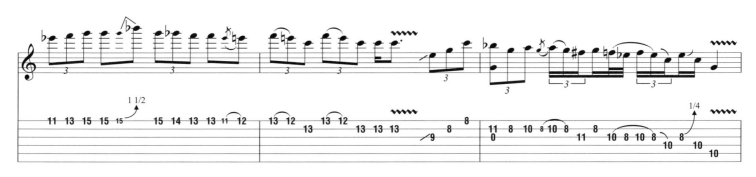

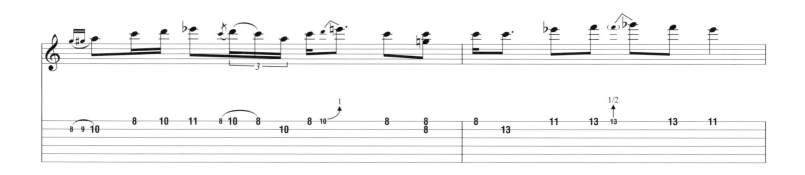

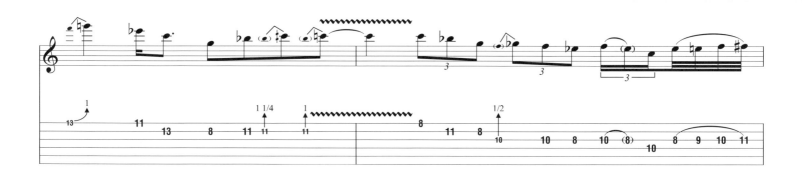

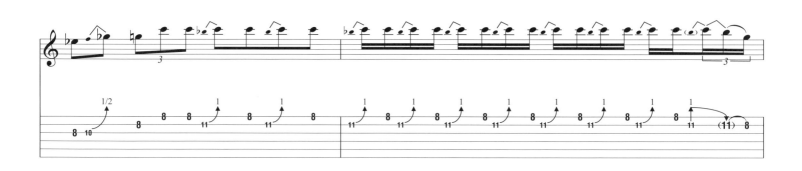

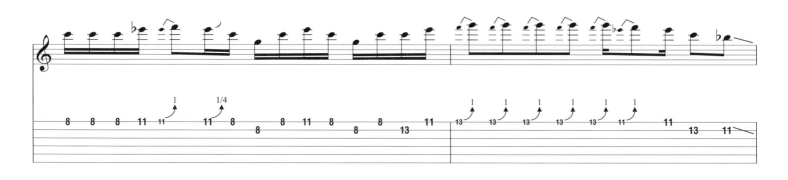

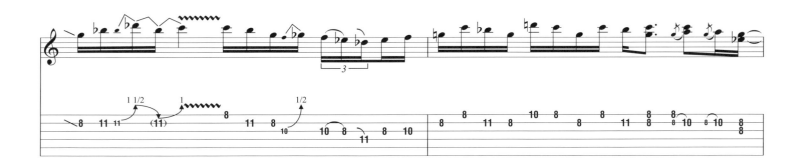

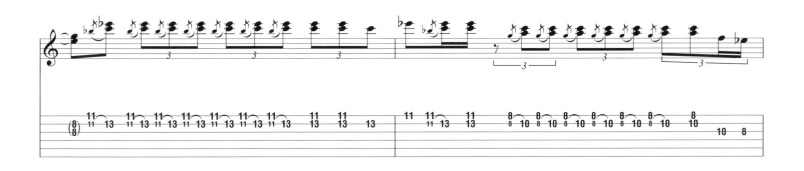

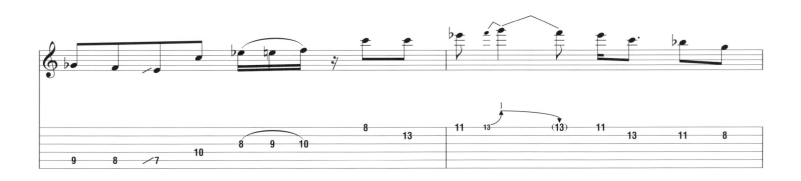

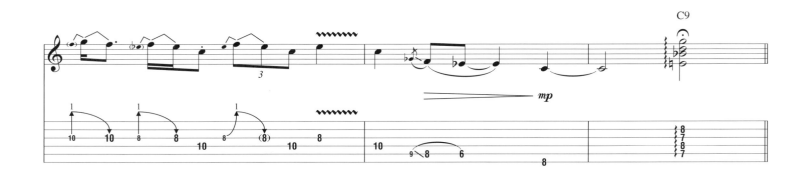

Example 39
(1:46)

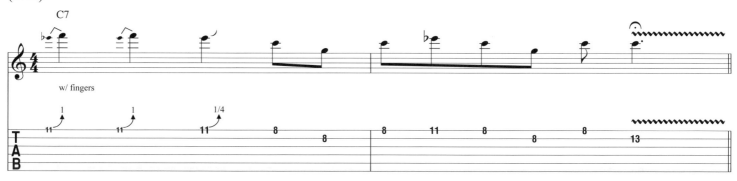

Example 40
(1:53)

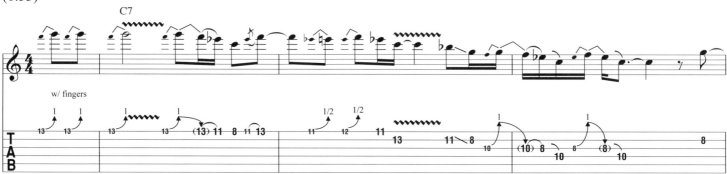

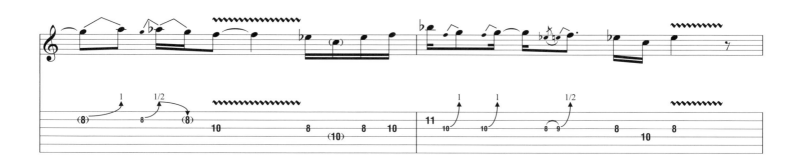

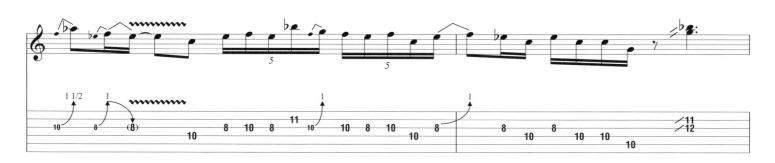

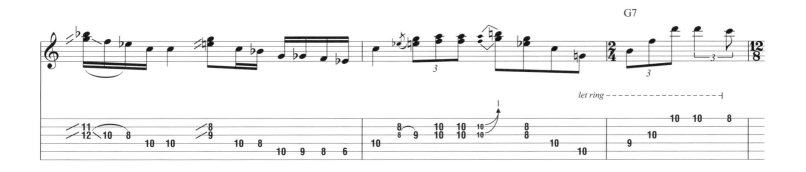

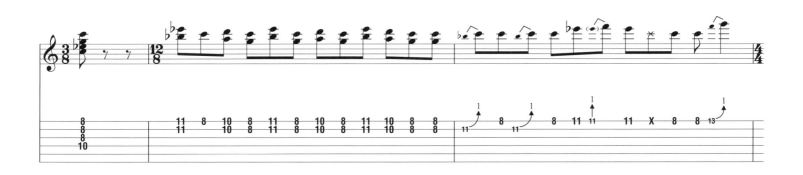

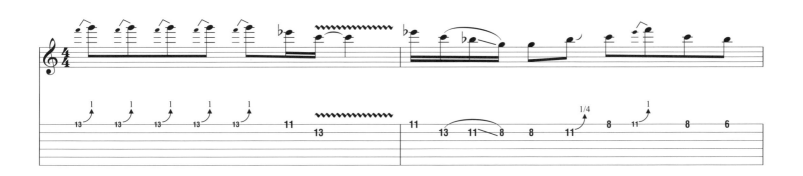

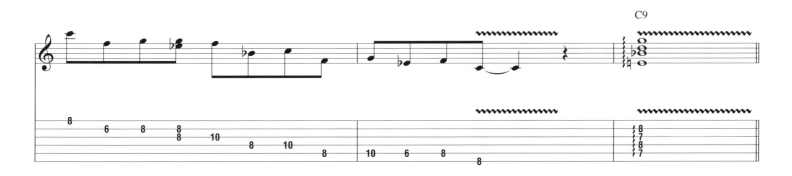

GUITAR NOTATION LEGEND

Guitar music can be notated three different ways: on a *musical staff*, in *tablature*, and in *rhythm slashes*.

RHYTHM SLASHES are written above the staff. Strum chords in the rhythm indicated. Use the chord diagrams found at the top of the first page of the transcription for the appropriate chord voicings. Round noteheads indicate single notes.

THE MUSICAL STAFF shows pitches and rhythms and is divided by bar lines into measures. Pitches are named after the first seven letters of the alphabet.

TABLATURE graphically represents the guitar fingerboard. Each horizontal line represents a string, and each number represents a fret.

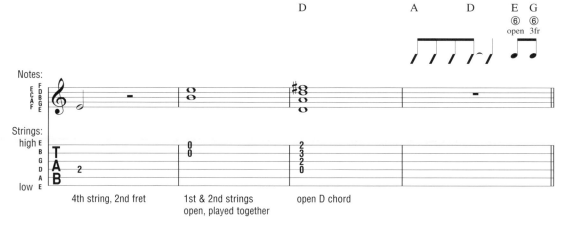

4th string, 2nd fret

1st & 2nd strings open, played together

open D chord

Definitions for Special Guitar Notation

HALF-STEP BEND: Strike the note and bend up 1/2 step.

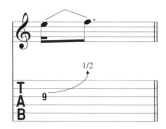

WHOLE-STEP BEND: Strike the note and bend up one step.

GRACE NOTE BEND: Strike the note and immediately bend up as indicated.

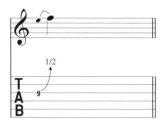

SLIGHT (MICROTONE) BEND: Strike the note and bend up 1/4 step.

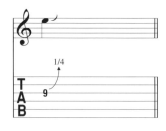

BEND AND RELEASE: Strike the note and bend up as indicated, then release back to the original note. Only the first note is struck.

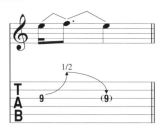

PRE-BEND: Bend the note as indicated, then strike it.

PRE-BEND AND RELEASE: Bend the note as indicated. Strike it and release the bend back to the original note.

UNISON BEND: Strike the two notes simultaneously and bend the lower note up to the pitch of the higher.

VIBRATO: The string is vibrated by rapidly bending and releasing the note with the fretting hand.

WIDE VIBRATO: The pitch is varied to a greater degree by vibrating with the fretting hand.

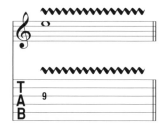

HAMMER-ON: Strike the first (lower) note with one finger, then sound the higher note (on the same string) with another finger by fretting it without picking.

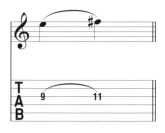

PULL-OFF: Place both fingers on the notes to be sounded. Strike the first note and without picking, pull the finger off to sound the second (lower) note.

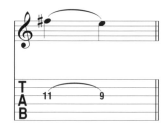

LEGATO SLIDE: Strike the first note and then slide the same fret-hand finger up or down to the second note. The second note is not struck.

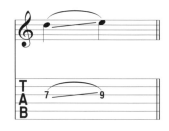

SHIFT SLIDE: Same as legato slide, except the second note is struck.

TRILL: Very rapidly alternate between the notes indicated by continuously hammering on and pulling off.

TAPPING: Hammer ("tap") the fret indicated with the pick-hand index or middle finger and pull off to the note fretted by the fret hand.

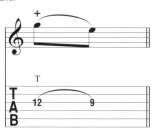

NATURAL HARMONIC: Strike the note while the fret-hand lightly touches the string directly over the fret indicated.

Harm.

T
A 12
B

PINCH HARMONIC: The note is fretted normally and a harmonic is produced by adding the edge of the thumb or the tip of the index finger of the pick hand to the normal pick attack.

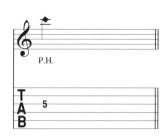

P.H.

T
A 5
B

HARP HARMONIC: The note is fretted normally and a harmonic is produced by gently resting the pick hand's index finger directly above the indicated fret (in parentheses) while the pick hand's thumb or pick assists by plucking the appropriate string.

8va

H.H.

T
A 7(19)
B

PICK SCRAPE: The edge of the pick is rubbed down (or up) the string, producing a scratchy sound.

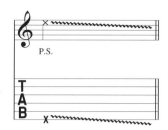

P.S.

T
A
B X

MUFFLED STRINGS: A percussive sound is produced by laying the fret hand across the string(s) without depressing, and striking them with the pick hand.

T
A X
B X

PALM MUTING: The note is partially muted by the pick hand lightly touching the string(s) just before the bridge.

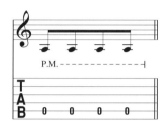

P.M.

T
A
B 0 0 0 0

RAKE: Drag the pick across the strings indicated with a single motion.

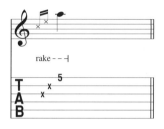

rake

T
A 5
B x x

TREMOLO PICKING: The note is picked as rapidly and continuously as possible.

T
A 5 7
B

ARPEGGIATE: Play the notes of the chord indicated by quickly rolling them from bottom to top.

T 5
A 5
B 5

VIBRATO BAR DIVE AND RETURN: The pitch of the note or chord is dropped a specified number of steps (in rhythm), then returned to the original pitch.

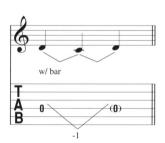

w/ bar

T
A 0 (0)
B
-1

VIBRATO BAR SCOOP: Depress the bar just before striking the note, then quickly release the bar.

w/ bar

T
A 4 5 7
B

VIBRATO BAR DIP: Strike the note and then immediately drop a specified number of steps, then release back to the original pitch.

-1/2 -1/2 -1/2

w/ bar

-1/2 -1/2 -1/2

T
A 7 7 7
B

Additional Musical Definitions

(accent)	•	Accentuate note (play it louder).
(accent)	•	Accentuate note with great intensity.
(staccato)	•	Play the note short.
⊓	•	Downstroke
∨	•	Upstroke

D.S. al Coda • Go back to the sign (%), then play until the measure marked "*To Coda*," then skip to the section labelled "**Coda**."

D.C. al Fine • Go back to the beginning of the song and play until the measure marked "*Fine*" (end).

Rhy. Fig. • Label used to recall a recurring accompaniment pattern (usually chordal).

Riff • Label used to recall composed, melodic lines (usually single notes) which recur.

Fill • Label used to identify a brief melodic figure which is to be inserted into the arrangement.

Rhy. Fill • A chordal version of a Fill.

tacet • Instrument is silent (drops out).

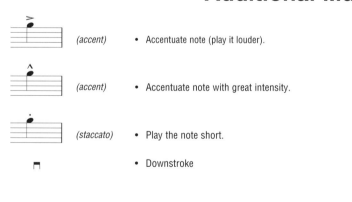

• Repeat measures between signs.

• When a repeated section has different endings, play the first ending only the first time and the second ending only the second time.

NOTE: Tablature numbers in parentheses mean:
1. The note is being sustained over a system (note in standard notation is tied), or
2. The note is sustained, but a new articulation (such as a hammer-on, pull-off, slide or vibrato) begins, or
3. The note is a barely audible "ghost" note (note in standard notation is also in parentheses).

HOT LICKS

For the first time, the legendary Hot Licks guitar instruction video series is being made available in book format with online access to the classic video footage. All of the guitar tab from the original video booklets has been re-transcribed and edited using modern-day technology to provide you with the most accurate transcriptions ever created for this series. Plus, we've included tab for examples that were previously not transcribed, providing you with the most comprehensive Hot Licks guitar lessons yet.

THE LEGENDARY GUITAR OF JASON BECKER

This re-transcribed and edited book with online video includes guitar tab and new, accurate transcriptions. It features footage collected from Becker's 1989 guitar clinic at the Atlanta Institute of Music (AIM), a clinic from Japan, his famous "yo-yo" live guitar solo, rare home video, various television news items and more. Topics covered include: Becker's use of the Japanese scale, pentatonic ideas, arpeggios and sweep picking, his "triangle pattern," sections of his original song "Serrana" and more.

14048279 Book/Online Video......................... $19.99

GEORGE BENSON – THE ART OF JAZZ GUITAR

In this edition, ten-time Grammy Award® winner George Benson covers chord substitution, turnarounds, the Wes Montgomery style, and more. He demonstrates his signature scat-style singing on "This Masquerade" and soloing over the "On Broadway" vamp. It also includes several virtuoso solo jazz and blues guitar performances. The video is accessed online using the unique code found inside the book and can be streamed or downloaded.

14048278 Book/Online Video......................... $19.99

JAMES BURTON – THE LEGENDARY GUITAR

Guitarist James Burton (Ricky Nelson, Elvis Presley) covers a wide range of classic rock 'n' roll and country-style guitar skills and techniques heard on such timeless rock hits as "Susie-Q," "Travelin' Man" and "Fools Rush In," among others. You'll learn: hybrid picking, steel guitar licks, string bending technique, chicken pickin', bending behind the nut, cross-string picking, his "echo effect" rhythm style, and more.

00269774 Book/Online Video......................... $19.99

BUDDY GUY – TEACHIN' THE BLUES

This book/video provides a unique chance to learn from the greatest Chicago blues guitarist of them all. In these video lessons, Buddy Guy reveals what he learned from such legends as Jimmy Reed, T-Bone Walker, and Lightnin' Hopkins, among others. Includes 40 transcribed examples. You'll learn: 9th chord riffs and licks, playing lead style with fingers, how to emulate slide guitar, boogie riffs, piano-style rhythms, and much more.

00253934 Book/Online Video......................... $19.99

WARREN HAYNES – ELECTRIC BLUES & SLIDE GUITAR

In this edition, guitarist Warren Haynes (Gov't Mule, Allman Brothers Band) covers a wide range of blues-rock and slide guitar skills and techniques, including phrasing, vibrato, string bending, and soloing as well as mixing major and minor scales, using space, and exploiting those blue notes within intervals. You'll learn: attack and vibrato, string bending technique, playing outside the blues scale, fingerpicking slide guitar, damping techniques, slide vibrato and intonation, and more.

00261616 Book/Online Video......................... $19.99

ERIC JOHNSON – TOTAL ELECTRIC GUITAR

This re-transcribed and edited book with online video includes guitar tab and new, accurate transcriptions. Techniques and approaches are presented in this Eric Johnson master class including the styles of Jimi Hendrix, Eric Clapton, Wes Montgomery, Chet Atkins, Jerry Reed, Jeff Beck and more. Topics covered include: picking techniques, pentatonic phrasing, left- and right-hand muting, pedal steel-style bends, unique chord voicings, harmonics, and more.

14048277 Book/Online Video......................... $19.99

BRENT MASON – NASHVILLE CHOPS & WESTERN SWING GUITAR

Nashville session legend Brent Mason takes you through a dazzling array of techniques and styles. You'll learn: chicken pickin' for rhythm and lead, Jerry Reed style, unique bends, double stops, banjo-style licks, claw style, drop D licks, Western swing licks, and much more!

14047858 Book/Online Video......................... $19.99

THE GUITAR OF BRIAN SETZER

This volume provides a unique chance to learn from guitarist Brian Setzer. Get one-on-one insights on his approach to rockabilly, blues, jazz, and country, including wild string-bending techniques, slap-echo effects, and hot solos. You'll learn Setzer's favorite: rockabilly rhythms, single-string "bop" runs, double-stop riffs, chord substitutions, rockabilly fingerpicking, and much more.

00269775 Book/Online Video......................... $19.99

HAL•LEONARD®

1118
020